STAND-UP
POETRY

Performance poems with teeth

edited by Fraser Grace

f r a m e w o r k s

FRAMEWORKS
38 De Montfort Street, Leicester LE1 7GP, England

First published 1991

British Library Cataloguing in Publication Data
Stand-up poetry: performance poems with teeth.
1. Poetry in English, 1945– – Anthologies
I. Grace, Fraser
821.91408

ISBN 0–85111–217–X

Set in Linotron Palatino
Photoset by Parker Typesetting Service, Leicester
Printed in Great Britain by Cox & Wyman Ltd,
Reading, Berks

Frameworks is an imprint of Inter-Varsity Press, the book-publishing division of the Universities and Colleges Christian Fellowship.

CONTENTS

Introduction

'Known words grow wings; print springs and shoots; the voice discovers the poet's ear; it's found that a poem on a page is only half a poem.'

These words, from Dylan Thomas speaking at a Festival of Spoken Poetry, have proved a useful guide while sifting through the verses for this collection.

One of the chief aims of *Stand-up poetry* is to stimulate the performance of poetry without endangering the life of the reader. This is no easy task, since in my experience the word 'poetry' is often regarded as the death-knell of all that is interesting. In addition, what passes for performance verse often falls apart when it manifests itself in print. Having spent many happy hours ranting to my heart's content, I am now confident not only that these poems will sprout wings as soon as they are read aloud, but also, that each poem will only be discovered to have been 'half a poem' *after* it has been heard; on the page, the poem looks solid enough, but when 'spoken' it unnervingly becomes twice the poem it was. This is a testimony to the craft of the poets represented here, and a suitable challenge for those who would perform their poems.

In setting out the poems I have played it literally by ear. The five sections of 'rock', 'soul', 'pop', 'blues' and 'gospel' are not intended to be of any great significance, other than to distinguish loosely between moods and angle of attack. This is particularly true when it comes to the 'gospel' section; 'The Gospel' itself – referring to the good news of Jesus – is as likely to turn up in the rock section as anywhere else; in contrast, 'gospel' here refers to the mood or atmosphere of celebration, reminiscent of gospel music, which usually centres around some aspect of God's love.

It should also be noted that, in common with their musical namesakes, there is considerable overlap between the styles suggested, and some very furry edges. Hopefully though, these categories will prove useful in constructing a live 'set' which has variety, progression and self-preservation, built-in.

One way to build such a set, or short programme of poems, would be to begin with an attention-grabbing up-tempo number from the 'rock' category, follow it with another because you fluffed the first, move on to a more reflective piece from the 'soul' group, plumb the depths with something from the 'blues', redeem the situation with a bit of 'pop' ('more light than bite') and leave the audience with a shower of gospel glory. In the process, you might also manage to slip in a poem of your own, and so share a stage with Stewart Henderson, Steve Turner, Evangeline Paterson, or any of the other poets here, at remarkably little additional expense.

It was a biography of Thomas Hardy which provided me with a second guiding principle for *Stand-up poetry*, when it quoted these words: 'The ultimate aim of the poet should be to touch our hearts by showing his own.'

Not all the poems here express an overt gospel message, but all are written by Christians, and can be used to touch the listener's heart. This freedom to explore the whole range of emotions experienced by Christians offers us the chance to produce a set which is an honest, incisive tool, rather than a dogmatic bludgeon. These poems are not intended to be once and for all theological statements, but are primarily reflections on, or reactions to, common experience, and should be treated accordingly.

Finally, a more contemporary poet and broadcaster, Nigel Forde, helped me to narrow a seemingly boundless task, when he spoke of poetry as being where 'every line begins with a capital letter. Or not.'

I have found this definition to be of immense help during the compilation of our book, which I hope will in turn prove useful to you.

Fraser Grace

Stand-up poetry

It's a hot and sweaty, smoked-out dug-out of a dog-breath bar that you face. Alone. And all that's between you, you and them, is a microphone . . .

Or it's a crowd of brow-beaten dust-bummed barely awake boot-boys in black blazers blowing noses bored to high heaven but won't hear a word of it, cough, thank you . . .

Or maybe they're unsure, these unsaved. The unknowing, uncared-for, ultimately undone religion-sick lost that are waiting behind that door . . .

And you're the one to do it. Go on, stand and deliver, *that* poem like the devil, *that* poem like love, *that* poem there, with words like angel spit, *that* poem, the one they remember like the first kiss, or the last smack from the only one who cared, *that* poem, the one that went like *that* and won't go away, rattling round their skulls like a pebble in a coke can. *That* poem. Give them that.

And let the poetry like the people, like the Man they killed, Stand Up.

Rock

the boat

thump the drum

brook no opposition

Five hundred million pounds

The Earl of Grosvenor
has five hundred million pounds.
He is honeymooning in Hawaii.
He has five hundred million pounds
and he still has to honeymoon
in the world.
He has married Natalia.
She is not my sort of girl.
Five hundred million pounds
and he marries someone
who is not my sort of girl.
The Earl of Grosvenor
carries a black case
in his right hand.
It is probably heavy.
He will probably sweat.
Damp patches will form
beneath his arms
as if he were a construction worker
or an unemployed gentleman
carrying a black case.
I expect his shoes hurt sometimes.
I expect he forgets his handkerchief.
I expect he wonders whether Natalia
really loves him.
I expect he wonders what it would be like
to only have four hundred and fifty
million pounds.

The Earl of Grosvenor takes off.
He wonders whether the engines will catch fire.
He knows you can't pay engines off.
He knows that the ocean is indifferent to millionaires.
Five hours in the air and he is restless.
Five hundred million pounds and he is restless.

Steve Turner

Mr Adam

tell me Mr Adam
how does your garden grow
– with warning bells and nuclear shells
and Eve on video

with pinstripe yuppie businessmen
a-standing in a row
with hamburgers and horoscopes
and all-night movie shows

with love in plain brown envelopes
from people you don't know
with grasping TV preachers
seeking profits here below

so tell me Mr Adam
how does your garden grow
– with warning bells and nuclear shells
and Eve on video

with concrete-covered landscapes
where toxic rivers flow
as girls and boys come out to play
beneath a neon glow

with Cain paid for talking
in a TV studio
where they play slow-motion replays

and you watch them blow by blow

so tell me Mr Adam
how does your garden grow
– with all the seeds you planted
a long long time ago

Mike Starkey

Death on a crossing

What he never thought to consider was whether
the thing was true. What bewildered him, mostly,
was the way the rumours had of reaching him
from such improbable sources – illiterate pamphlets
pressed in his hand, the brash or the floundering
    stranger
who came to his door, the proclamations, among
so many others, on hoardings
                      though sometimes waking
a brief dismay, that never quite prodded him
to the analyst's couch.
                      But annunciations, he thought,
should come to a rational man in a rational way.
He walked between a skyful of midnight angels
and a patch on somebody's jeans, both saying
the same thing to his stopped ears
                      till the day
when he stepped on a crossing with not enough
    conviction
to get him safe to the other side, and he lay
among strangers' feet, and the angels lowered their
    trumpets
and no sweet chariot swung, to carry him home.

Evangeline Paterson

Poem for the hard of hearing

This is a poem for the hard of hearing
listen, as it falls
Listen to the crash as it drops through the ceiling
and echoes   'choes   'choes
round the walls

These are the words to draw blood from your
      ear-drums
the vibrations will jarr-r-r at your spine
I said this is a poem for the hard of hearing
won't you listen this time?

These are the words to smash through your cranium
to misplace a heart beat-or-two
I said this is a poem for the hard of hearing
God   loves   You.

Fraser Grace

TV evangelist

You talk of commitment
Like a sales pitch
For a new herbal diet
A savings scheme
A personal pension plan
You make conversion
As radical
As joining Readers Digest
A change of heart
As easy
As a change of anti-perspirant
You offer the blessings of heaven
For the small investment
Of a simple tithe
And back it
With a guaranteed return

You leave no room for questions
For doubts
For honesty
You hire satelite time
To tell foreigners how to live
And rage your righteousness
Through a million cables
Back home.

You are the ultra-bright
Might is right

Acceptable face of America

But be careful
The whiteness of your sepulchre
Is showing

Gerard Kelly

Poem for Putzi Hanfstaengel

Note: Putzi Hanfstaengel, pianist, wit and bon viveur, was a permanent fixture in Hitler's entourage. The Fuhrer relied on Hanfstaengel's urbane presence to disarm visitors from the outside world. Through sheer exercise of his charm, he survived Hitler's increasing disenchantment with him, and escaped to America, where he lived to a respected old age.

Clowning on the margin
of history's pages,
playing the piano for
your very good friend,
clever man, funny man,
nice-to-have-around man,
   oh Putzi Hanfstaengel
   play for us again!

The ride you went along for
ended on the rapids.
You bobbed like a cork and
you floated back again.
Now, on the telly screen,
soft-spoken, charming,
   oh Putzi Hanfstaengel
   play for us again!

Play it for us, like you
played it for Adolf,

and when it's time to go, boy,
you'd better play it then!
Outside the door six
million ghosts are waiting.
   oh Putzi Hanfstaengel,
   clever Putzi Hanfstaengel,
   fun Putzi Hanfstaengel,
   better swing it then!

Evangeline Paterson

The bran man cometh

With a fist full of wheatgerm he flies through the sky
wanna tell you that's the Bran Man
that's right, I said he is the Bran Man
and he's saving the world with his bon apetite
I said he is the Bran Man / and the Bran Man's alright

'cos he got brown rice in his moustache
and no shoes on his toes
and he wears whole-wool jumpers
wherever he goes
he got them pulses, they're pulsating,
he got free-range, and it shows
'cos he wears Vegan trousers
and eats that cashew roast

I'm talkin' about the Bran Man / and the Bran Man's
    alright

And he says
Eat your wheatgerm and you'll feel OK
Digest and survive, that is the natural way
There's a Nutrition-Free Zone and it's headed this
    way!
Stick with the Man with Bran left in
Listen brother
He's the answer to everything

Alright

With a side dish of salad he flies to your side
wanna tell you that's the Bran Man
Gonna take you a walk on the walnut side
I said he is the Bran Man / and the Bran Man's alright

'cos he got friendly with the trendies
gotta keep their brains lead-free
from the Wrights and the Webers
to the aristocracy
He got a grip upon this nation
he gotta grip on you and me
Gotta grip on ruffage, baby
gonna set our bowels free

I'm talkin' about the Bran Man / and the Bran Man's
        alright

And he says
Eat your wheatgerm and you'll feel OK
Digest and survive, that is the natural way
There's a Nutrition-Free Zone and it's headed this
        way
stick with the Man with Bran left in
That's wild, honey
He's the answer to everything

Alright.

Fraser Grace

Prehistories

1 Dinosaur

Muscle-bound bruiser of the swamp,
with both brains on the blink,
what chance did I have against
the soft-furred cunning of
higher orders under my feet,
tripping me up as I stumbled
through the forest? How could I compete
in a changing swamp with the climate
of opinion turned against big
and snow piled around my eggs?
So at last, feet hurting, I dropped
exhausted to the earth, and my veins
turned to glaciers of cold blood.

2 Neanderthal

As for me, your average hairy
troglodyte with hooded eyes
like a troll in a fairy tale,
it was advances in technology
and a skull one size too small
made me redundant, the market for
my chipped stones crashing when
what folk wanted was bronze, iron,
plastics, micro-chips: a future
invested in the atom age.

My old flint knives could cut no ice;
I shut up my cave and shuffled off.

3 Homo Sapiens

The star at the top of the tree
has learnt to fly off on his own.
Poet, scientist, engineer,
all the right qualities
for taking the universe by storm.
When I fly higher than the birds,
my feet never touch the ground.
But a head in the clouds can't see
the earth spinning round beneath.
There's nothing I couldn't produce,
given time and the right materials.
When I blow up in your faces,
I'm taking the rest of you with me.

Steven Waling

Born again

Inna dis countree
everybody Christain.
De Butcher, de Baker, de Policeman
Whaat, de Policeman –
Yes, mi dear
every living soul!
At first, me tink sey:
'What a blested island'
Til
Mi realize dat
Not everybody
Born Again.

Dem nar tink twice
Fi work on Sunday –
Go party Saturday night –
Were dem dere fi all night prayer Friday?
Thursday Bible study – mi never see them –
Mi mout woulda drop fi see dem a choir practice on
        Wednesday –
Intercessory prayer Tuesday – seat dem empty!
Monday, just lickle an few come fi praise de Lawd –
Hmm.
Yet – dem a Christain?

But, nar Born Again.

'Yu speak inna tongue?'

Dem look pon mi like mi mad.
'Holy Spirit inna yu?'
Mi hear dem enquire if a new drink?
'De Lawd yur personal Saviour?'
Blinkin dem eye – dem nar answer.
'Yu baptize inna water?'
Dem sey dem christen when dem born.
'We is Christain' dem shout.
Is dem Born Again?

Mi heart bruck –
An sadness fill me up.
To tink
To imagine
Dat
Dem nar fully understood
Jesus
When him sey
Fi a man fi enter heaven
He must be Born Again.

Millie Murray

The news and weather

A man shot a man who shot a man who shot a man
Said it wasn't murder it just went off in his hand
We got a bigger bomb than the one we had before
On the Middle East border there wasn't any score
Some people starved to death in a city far away
A man in a suit will read the weather for today
A man in a suit will read the weather for today

A spokesman said he could not comment at the time
A friend of a friend said the rumour was a lie
The next door neighbour always thought that he was
    funny
The man who guessed the draw was given lots of
    money
The corrupt M.P. said he'd nothing more to say
A man in a suit will read the weather for today
A man in a suit will read the weather for today

The star of thirty films has just cast his fifth wife
The man who killed children must stay indoors for
    life
The financial index is falling down again
Pence to the dollar to the mark to the yen
Tobacco and petrol and the price you'll have to pay
A man in a suit will read the weather for today
A man in a suit will read the weather for today

At the football match it was the crowd who went and
    lost
The team managers are trying to estimate the cost
The little girl went missing only three days ago
Don't travel by train because they're on a go-slow
A leading tennis player has admitted that he's gay
A man in a suit will read the weather for today
A man in a suit will read the weather for today

Policemen say watch out for strangers at your door
Ring this number if you've seen this man before
Another soldier died but he didn't have a girl
There's been a great disaster the biggest in the world
Yet down at the zoo the woolly bears come out to
    play
A man in a suit will read the weather for today
A man in a suit will read the weather for today

A two minute warning will follow this newscast
You'll hear a high pitched noise, then you'll hear a
    blast
The windows will go missing, you'll be blinded by a
    light
But if you remain calm everything will be alright
Some of you may notice that your skin will peel away
A man in a suit will read the weather for today
A man in a suit will read the weather for today.

Steve Turner

Somewhere in suburbia

she'd have had her mother's eyes
but she never had her heart
she'd have had her father's smile
but he couldn't spare the time

she could have been a radical
a twice-born evangelical
she could have had her photo
on her grandmother's wall

but the doctors get their money
and the nurses change the bedclothes
and somewhere in suburbia
there'll be one less mouth to feed

King Herod sits in Harley Street
the land of milk and honey
while his bankers in the counting house
are counting out the money

a doctor puts his raincoat on
the nurses hurry home
the Maker gets his image back
a girl drives home alone

now the doctors get their money
and the nurses change the bedclothes

and somewhere in suburbia
there'll be one less mouth to feed

Mike Starkey

There was no

There was no grave grave enough
to ground me
to mound me
I broke the balm then slit the shroud
wound round me
that bound me

There was no death dead enough
to dull me
to cull me
I snapped the snake and waned his war
to lull me
to null me

there was no cross cross enough
to nil me
to still me
I hung as gold that bled, and bloomed
A rose that rose and prised the tomb
away from Satan's wilful doom
There was no cross, death, grave
or room
to hold me.

Stewart Henderson

woo my

Soul

apart

When the war is over

when the war is over we will
seem so strange even to ourselves

when the war is over
we will not be concerned about
leaving our doors open

we will not need doors
we will not need walls
not even
the walls
of our flesh

our language will become a midnight babble
a millennium will seem
a midsummer night's dream

the name of Jesus becomes the air we breathe

we will transport to Mars
as easily as
the spirit of God
broods and moves over the waters

each risen through a land of forgotten cloud

when the war is over

until then we are blessed
by a happy sadness, by a loving sorrow
until then
the testing of tragedy and the hours of grace

a gentle spirit behind a time-worn face.

Alex Warner

The ballad of Bertha Bailey

Big and burly Bertha Bailey
wears B.O. and Brut
but she has a second sylph-like self
who wears a sailor suit
See her rise above the roof-tops
in search of macho men
she lures them lithely from their bedrooms
then bounces them back again

She'll not have Harry
   He says I'm hefty
She'll not favour Fred
   He says I'm foul
Oh there'll never be a boy for Bertha Bailey
   though I once was the darling of them all
she says
   I once was the darlin' of them all

Blushingly blousey Louise Bertha Bailey
alights from the bus in Bakerloo Square
She looks seventeen in her silver silk stockings
she looks like the girl with the Silvikrin hair
For she knows she may meet the man she might
      marry
and she's anxious to seem oh so sensuously soft
But it's not Mr Right who will reap what she's
      rendered
not Mr Right who so courteously coughed

Now she's pinned to a wall by a wild arm so weighty
and she's flinging her fists at a fat face so foul
And she's dying to die, she feels so damn dirty
can hardly believe no-one's hearing her howl

Louise Bertha Bailey all bruised, bashed and broken
staggers for somewhere to silently sit
She finds a hot cafe, orders four helpings
starts eating certain she'll make herself sick
But daylight is gradually down on her dawning
as she drifts from the door at the dark dead of night
I'll be fat, I'll be foul, I will feed till I'm forty
and I'll be safe and as sound as a sow in their sight

Then I'll not have to have Harry
He'll say I'm too heavy
not have to fear Fred
He'll say I'm so foul
then there'll never be a boy for Bertha Bailey
I'll not be the darlin' of them all, she said
I'll never be the darling of them all

Big and burly Bertha Bailey
wears B.O. and Brut
but she has a second sylph-like self
who wears a sailor suit
See her rise above the roof-tops
in search of macho men
she lures them lithely from their bedrooms
then bounces them back again

Fraser Grace

Clown

clown
only asked for laughter
but they painted him
as someone else

only asked to tumble
but they pushed him over
flat on his face

only asked if he could smile
but now he grimaces
in greasepaint

only asked for love
but they want him
to be amused

clown
only asked only asked
but now he
never questions

Rupert Loydell

Survival day

It should have been
a more momentous occasion.
There should have been some act,
some symbol
to mark the moment when you passed
from tenuous anonymity
to the legal certainty of personhood,
when you inherited
the protection of the living and crossed the boundary
between merciful destruction
and murder.

There should have been a ceremony
to herald your survival.

But there was
no ceremony.
There were no crowds.
No telegrams were sent.
No-one even noticed
when the first day of your twenty-ninth week began
just as the last of your twenty-eighth had ended:
with the furious rushing of blood,
the racing of your pulse
and the constant soporific rhythm
of that other heart, beating.

The gentle, amber fluid
of life.
The soft, lapping fluid
of safety.

Gerard Kelly

In the pigsty

The Prodigal, pale with worry and cold
his lips cracked, his eyes bold from his skin, and
not quite sure if his concentration played
tricks with his mind, lay outstretched
and contemplated without conclusion.

Round him the end products of his riches –
'Amelia, the Pig' butting him from behind,
'Constance' spraying mud from her scew hooves,
'Jessica' – he knew a girl called Jessica once –
listlessly pushing as he scooped his food.

But there was something he longed to recall,
somewhere and someone, a faint smell of hay;
it was all too much – he returned to the
pigs, fed them with memories, dreams and
        prospects.

The pigs left the swill, and soon he felt full.

Gerald Kells

Hip-op rappity rap

I'm sitting here on the fourteenth floor
in the limb replacement corridor
my X-ray of some months before
confirms just why this leg's so sore,
and I've begged the femur specialist
to eradicate my starboard list
'Please operate, make this ache desist'
he said, 'Take these pills, join the waiting list'

he put me down
he put me down
he put me down
he put me down
for a

Hip-op rappity rap
I can't stand straight, I'm a lop-sided chap
Hip-op rappity roo
My career is ended as a kangaroo
Hip-op rappity squeaks
It's not much fun when your pelvis creaks
Hip-op rappity ouch
only three more years of pain to go
and again

Hip-op rappity rap

They'd treat me quick if I had something mean

Like Egyptian typhoid or a ruptured spleen
But all I've got is a permanent lean
I make Long John Silver look like Torvill and Dean
They said 'If you go private there's a room for you
with colour television and a tree-top view
or why not do it yourself at B & Q
with a saw and a ratchet and some super glue?'

I couldn't pay
I couldn't pay
I couldn't pay
I couldn't pay
for a

Hip-op rappity rap

Stewart Henderson

Awakening

Eyes still full of dreams
squeezing out the last drops of darkness
allowing the slow steady streams of sunshine
to fill the void.
Body, aching with lifetimes of
curled defensiveness,
stretching strangely and rediscovering
familiar form and freedom.
Mind, dusty shelves of once-read books
creaking open.
Spirit, new-born infant
sucking air into lungs whose existence
it had hardly dared hope for.
Breath which expands, searches out,
saturates.
Breath which has its own birth in
Love
for you which once was sleeping and now awakes.

Michele Taylor

Never-never land

there's instant buying-power
with six months to repay
and a man who deals in easy terms
is just a call away
the waiting's gone from wanting
the credit's on demand
our dreams become reality
in never-never land

I bargain-hunt therefore I am
and pay in monthly sums
every day is market day
tomorrow never comes
with the Joneses on my mind
and a wallet in my hand
I'm in the pink and born to shop
in never-never land

plastic makes the world go round
the slow get left behind
need a loan? pick up the phone
while tomorrow's out of mind
    but seasons changed, tomorrow's here
much sooner than you planned
the water's deep and sharks have teeth
in never-never land

the brylcream voice, the plastic smile
the million words for 'spend'
give way before the thumbscrew frown
of an inflexible friend
the man stands at the doorstep
the timer's out of sand
the small print's looming larger
in never-never land

shop windows wink at passers-by
and beckon them inside
all the towns are painted red
no fantasy denied
the people build their house of cards
and try to make it stand
while the bailiff comes a-knocking
in never-never land

Mike Starkey

Smudged

The smudged dusk of
children's eyeshadow
on summer evenings

The first hot
long days of touch
where we used to play
and while away the evenings.

Now it's
'do I look alright?'
and
'. . . be back later . . .'

The eyeshadow children
loiter in the evenings
wondering what to do
with their bodies.

What to do with
their long hot summers,
already fading
to dark . . .

Rupert Loydell

In the aftermath

Sundrenched village
sleeping uneasily
in the aftermath.
Nervous children
on patrol
with rifles
as big
as themselves,
innocence
snatched away
by crisis.
Tension mounts
as heat rises.
Waiting.

Mark Reaney

Pop

more light

than bite

Smiling in a built up area

Caught red-handed
smiling in a built up area.
Not even
a sly smirk
or a leer
but a fully-fledged
no holds barred
beam
in a grey Friday
bank queue.
Please excuse us
for sharing something
of the joy of living
in a public place
without a permit.

Mark Reaney

Mary he said

think of me
when the surf is pounding the shoreline Mary
he said

wait for me
and I shall bring you perfumes
and many jewels
the colour of your eyes Mary
he said

never forget me
and when the child grows tell him he has
a father who loves him dearly Mary
he said

watch for me
and when I return I shall bring him tales of
sea beasts, reefs and treasures Mary
he said

trust me
and if they say a sailor
has a girl in every port
say you don't believe their lies Mary
he said

the name's Alison
she said

Mike Starkey

Gang rules

Let's form a gang, just you and me
jelly for breakfast, cornflakes for tea
Let's do things that grown-ups can't do
put clothes on backwards, unlock the zoo

Let's form a gang, just she and he
swim like a lapwing over the sea
Let's throw healing at pains far too deep
confetti at funerals, no more sleep

Let's form a gang, just thou and me
a bucket and spade versus the scree
Let's wear snow shoes when the sun burns bright
then ask the Queen if she cries at night.

Stewart Henderson

Leftright

In the year 1870
the Grand Duchy of Lichtenstein
sent eighty men
(leftright leftright
in their long overcoats)
and one cannon
to the Franco-Prussian War

and when the war was over
welcomed home again
(leftright leftright)
eighty-one men
and one cannon

no-one has ever
accounted for this

Evangeline Paterson

Spare rib

God made de light
To shine out bright
Him call it day – and de darkness night!
Den Him call fi water
Fi separate de space
Put de sea out so
And de land inna place!
Den de Lawd was pleased at what Him do,
So next –
Him bring forth grass and every plant too!
Sun and moon and stars Him make
But –
Even den Him never tek one break!
When Him look inna de sea
Him find it bare
So Him put some fish and creatures dere.
De same ting Him sey bout de empty land
So him make livestock
An den Him make Man –
– Him create every ting on dis earth
An ME
Him make fram a spare rib!

Millie Murray

Teardrops in my muesli

I see your face in the tofu spread
your smile between my prunes
I hear your voice in all our discs
of Kenyan noseflute tunes
we took the roughage with the smooth
as all young lovers do
but now teardrops in my muesli
tell me that we're through

you always seemed so full of beans
and I gave you free range
but you said we had problems
even wholefoods couldn't change
I'm still a Friend of Planet Earth
but I'd rather be friends with you
and teardrops in my muesli
tell me that we're through

the sparkle's gone from Perrier
the buzz has gone from bees
the odour's gone from the compost heap
and the armadillo cheese
every fibre of my body's
turned from green to blue
now teardrops in my muesli
tell me that we're through

Mike Starkey

Blues

mourning and weeping

in this vale of tears

I keep my spirit kicking

Speak

The microphone hordes advance.
They are brisk and shining. Their words
rattle like hail.

'How do you feel, Mrs Tyrwhitt,
Mrs Pentague, Mrs Blewitt,
now that your son is killed?
Do you want revenge?'

                    We sit
in our cardigans and aprons,
the photograph at our elbows.
We are diffident and slow.

'How does it feel, Mr Whittaker,
to be disabled . . . Mr Comstock,
to lose your sight? Are you bitter?'

We sit there, turning over
our huge unaccustomed grief.
The words are slow to come.

The microphones insist.
The faceless millions wait.

'How do you feel,
Mr and Mrs Golightly,
now that your child is missing?'

What should we say? What
does the beetle say to the wheel,
the worm to the spade? Does the mown grass
speak?

Evangeline Paterson

Birmingham says sorry

Note: In June of 1984, a man named Eddy Newman, and his two dogs, were found dead in their flat in Handsworth, Birmingham. They had been dead for a year.

All over the city
we're not searching for a dead man,
not searching for a dead man
All over the city
we're not turning it upside down

Has anyone seen the man who is dead
the man who is lying face down on his bed?
Will you please not help us to find this man
we're trying not to find him as fast as we can

We've not looked in the factory yards,
we've not looked in the drains,
we've not looked in the tower blocks
and the morgue's just not the same
we've bodies, and bodies, and bodies right here
but we ain't got nobody who's been dead for a year

All over the city
we're not searching for a dead man
not searching for a dead man
All over the city
we're not turning it upside down

Is it the man with the gun?
No.
Is it the girl who just jumped?
No, No, No,
That ain't the dead man
The dead man's been dead for a year

Tracker dogs are not sniffing
Helicopters are not chopping
Investigators are not investigating
Bobby's are not bob-bob-bobbing
'cos the dead man hunt-seasons not here

All over the city,
we're not searching for a dead man,
not searching for a dead man
All over the city
we're not turning it upside down

Dead for a year and none of us noticed
now the ultimate wallflower don't smell so sweet
and some of us who'd not noticed
the dead man was missing
are noticing the dead man's stink in the street.

Dead man's dogs don't bark at the window
Dead man's dogs don't bark at the door
yet none of us un-dead noticed or wondered
what the dead man's dead dogs were deading well
not barking for

How did we find him?
How did we find them?

Super-sleuthing Scotland Yard men?
Legions of dedicated bobbing policemen?

No.
Dead man found dead, face down in his bed,
by a visiting cutting-off specialist
from the Gas Board

MAN DEAD IN FLAT FOR YEAR!
GAS FIRE WAS STILL BURNING!!

Spokesman said, If only a small amount
is involved in bills, it would
take us quite some time to cut off the
– DEAD?!?

All over the city
we're searching for dead men
searching for dead men
All over the city
we're turning their gas fires down

Now the moral of the story
of The Ultimate Wallflower
and the dead man's dead dog gas fire pong,
is run yourself up a killer of a gas bill

We may still find you dead in your bed
one bright morning
but it won't take us nearly
so long.

Fraser Grace

Tramp

This mad prophet
gibbers mid-traffic,
wringing his hands
whilst mouthing at heaven.

No messages for us.
His conversation is simply
a passage through time.
He points and calls.

Our uneven stares dissuade
approach. We fear him, his
matted hair, patched coat,
grey look from sleeping out.

We mutter among ourselves
and hope he keeps away. No
place for him in our heaven,
there it's clean, and empty.

Rupert Loydell

You told me to grow up

You told me to grow up
but you didn't tell me how
I wore my mother's shoes
put lipstick on my face
I grew a woman's body and I laid that body down
I thought I'd been an adult
you just said I'd been around
You told me to grow up
but you didn't tell me how

You told me to grow up
I never knew how
You said I had the right to choose
you chose
they took this woman's body
and they shook the baby out
You said I'd been an adult

You tell me time will heal
it won't
You tell me to forget
I can't

What you see is a grown up body now
where once there lived a child.

Fraser Grace

An old Andorran custom
questions the dead

*Note: One of the smallest countries in the world, Andorra –
thanks to its isolated location high in the pyranees – has
retained many of its ancient beliefs and customs, of which
questioning the deceased is one.*

I spoke to the dead, oiled sea-bird,
questioned the poisoned fish,
saw the finger-sized foetus
asked 'Dead one who killed you?'
And the dead gave me no answer
but the wind whispered
'You, you, you.'

I looked at the battered baby,
the man blown apart by a bomb,
the suicide pulled from the water
asked: 'Dead one, who killed you?'
And the dead gave me no answer
but the wind whispered
'You, you, you.'

I gazed at a sterile planet
– our erstwhile orbiting earth –
lifeless and pitted with craters
cried: 'Dead one, who killed you?'
And the dead gave me no answer

and there was no wind to whisper
'You, you, you.'

Peggy Poole

Join what?

'If you can't beat 'em join 'em: but join what?'
His eyes see nothing in this gloomy light
straining through into his sitting room;
but the depth of his question astounds me.

'I've come to see how you're getting on –'
'I manage. Mustn't let it get me down.
I sometimes feel like I don't want to wake.'
'I see.' A sort of conversation starts.

And stops. And starts again. He shifts and grips
his white stick, and asks from his wheelchair,
'If you can't beat 'em join 'em: but join what?'
For two solid years he's kept himself indoors.

I scan his bookshelves for a common theme:
two Bibles, thrillers; a sex manual?
Even the mystical books he can now
no longer read, are musty with powers

long disused. Those pictures on the wall,
those ivories collecting dust in corners,
are giant's toys against this shrunken man:
'If you can't beat 'em join 'em: but join what?'

His life's reduced to a chair, and a frame
round the loo to hold him while he pees;
I visit once a week, find nothing to say

and another fine way of saying it.

He keeps recycling his original question:
'If you can't beat 'em join 'em: but join what?'
Like asking the meaning of the universe:
I run through all my answers, walking home.

Steven Waling

Tribal homeland

Here is the world's bitter end. Wind
is always blowing. Small mud houses cling
to the ground, their tin roofs weighted with stones.

Earth is trampled, here,
hard as brick. The bleak eroded hill
looks down, offers no hope, deflects the weather.

Across the waste comes a woman walking, flat
feet on cracked earth, blanket blazing orange-
yellow, bright as anger, loud as a bugle

under the threatening sky.
Now all that sad music lapses out of key.
Something here is not going to die.

Evangeline Paterson

Above the dove of love

Above the dove of love
dropped all his sap
on the juiceless earth
and flew furiously
at our high, hollow hearts

Bones did not break
in this plummet,
all that fell were his feathers
like a fluttering crown

Afterwards, during the hermit
ceremony of death,
the sky came
and made soft
his waxed, wounded wings

Above, the dove of love
is known in
other orbits,
and even eagles
dare not approach.

Stewart Henderson

Gospel

lifts him

higher and higher

The fire comes

you are a wild bear who squeezes and crushes
you are a fearsome thunder rolling green across black
     your
claws crack the earth stars fall

like cigarette butts stubbed on the tray
the people fear what you have to say when
you're a firestorm. You're a wild wonderous spirit

all life is formed when you speak
living words breathing into the dust
forming frames where hearts pump

in cages of white like ivory
notched knotted ribbed lifeblood flowing
a river coursing our veins

you are a wild bear you are risk
beautiful is your strength in human temples
spirit-breath raises us up teaches us, great are your

claws sword-sharp scratching as you
cry war wild horses gallop
one horseman black, one horseman white

one horseman red in the darkest night
one horseman red as war declared
you are the servant-hearted Conqueror

the earth quakes the spirits wake
all hell boils over for heaven's sake
war in heaven war on earth

four horsemen gallop on dark dry earth.

Alex Warner

The very thought

I love the very thought of Heaven:
Where angels sing
In perfect, perpetual Choir Practice.
Where Father, Son, and Spirit
Rule, unchallenged,
And are honoured in full measure.
I love the very thought of Heaven:
But I was not made
To live there.

I was not made
To walk on clouds,
And bask eternally
In immaterial splendour.
I was made for this green planet:
This tight ball
Of infinite beauty,
Alive with the unending possibilities
Of His creative power.
I was made for the sunshine
That blazes through the veins of leaves,
And glints in the tiny, perfect back
Of a ladybird, crossing my arm.
I was made to be human
In this, most human place.
I was made for Earth:
The Earth is my home.

That's why I'm glad
That God, more than anyone,
Is a Friend of the Earth.
That he was prepared
To die for its restoration,
And that's why I'm glad
That the magnificent, jewelled foundations
Of the mighty Pearly Gates,
Will be anchored
Deeply and for ever
In the soil of Earth.

Gerard Kelly

Escapologist

You say he broke prisoners' chains
but couldn't break his own; why then
this speculation he performed
a trick Houdini never knew
by rising living from the tomb?

Houdini sank, chained inside
his thick glass tank like a gangster
who blabbed, to rise unbound to crowds
of adoring applause; no-one
was around to see Christ rise

but the rumour still persists:
witnesses rumble in a ground
once thought firm as the stars;
lives are suspiciously brand new.
Something has certainly occurred.

Houdini nailed his secrets down
to the grave from which he couldn't
escape – but look: God's secret walks
and we can learn his tricks
if we keep our eyes wide open

slip the key   beneath our tongue

Steven Waling

Shalom

Shalom is a poem
that harvests the raw beauty of words
And spins and weaves them
Into cloths and braids:
The vivid, adjectival colours
Of silk,
The tactile, verbal weave
Of rough cotton.
Shalom is a coat that fits,
A house that sits in the landscape,
Like a jewel set in gold.
Old stone, red tile,
dark wood.
It is fresh spring water
Grass as sharp as dry-cleaned curtains.
It is everything as it should be:
Backs
Not beaten,
Stomachs
Not hungry.
It is a reality that defies reduction,
and evades definition:
A silver shining eel
That hovers in perfect stillness in the water
But darts out of reach
As soon as you try to touch it.

Shalom
is the healing that comes
When the finger of God
Touches
The world that He has made.

Gerard Kelly

The annunciation

All that holy light gets in your eyes
till you can't tell what's happening:
    the angel comes, his tidings
ring on air like bells
long after they were tolled.

    And when he goes, he leaves
a feather in your belly, fear
like a myth embarking on its
long voyage into history:
                                nine months on
and the dream wakes up, bawling,
in a mess of muddy straw

as the angel's words
dance upon the tip of your tongue,
    flames
burning the roof of your mouth.

Steven Waling

Whose grave is the ocean

Whose grave is the ocean
whose roof gulls skim,
and wind thresh.
Whose words were soaked
and whose eyes
were dulled by salt.
Guided by stars
with hearts fixed on home,
whose inheritance was none.
Down beneath froth
with the tangled rust of glory;
beyond all horizons,
amongst the kingdom not their own.
The ocean shifts its weight
as if pushed by a prayer
and the sunken socket
eyes the surface broken light.

Whose grave is the ocean
whose resurrection sprays.
Whose trumpet cracks the water
with a gilded flash of joy.

Steve Turner

Bread and wine

intoxicated
under canvas of marquee
falling into the waiting arms
of my jesus army comrade

totally relaxed
unable to contain the reverie
of ecstasy

hearing bugles hoot in jubilation
mayhem wild in expectation
spawned in controversy
i glimpsed glory
from well travelled eyes

who dares wins
the pledge of the prodigal
the pride of being vulnerable
the fear of the lord

bread and wine
and clean hands raised
bread and wine
the power of praise
sacrificed from a willing heart

do this in memory of me said he

Alex Warner

The last enemy

And He Who each day
reveals a new masterpiece of sky
and Whose joy
can be seen in the eyelash of a child
Who when He hears of our smug indifference
can whisper an ocean into lashing fury
and talk tigers into padding roars
This my God
Whose breath is in the wings of eagles
Whose power is etched in the crags of mountains
It is He Whom I will meet
in Whose Presence I will find tulips and clouds
kneeling martyrs and trees
the whole vast praising of his endless creation
And He will grant the uniqueness
that eluded me
in my earthly bartering with Satan
That day when He will erase the painful gasps of my
    ego
and I will sink my face into the wonder of his
    glorylove
and I will watch as planets converse with sparrows
On that day
when death is finally dead

Stewart Henderson

Acknowledgments

All poems are copyright and appear by permission of their authors. The following poems have been published previously in books and the permission to include them here has been given by the copyright holders.

'Hip-op rappity rap', 'Gang rules' and 'Above the dove of love' are taken from *A Giant's Scrapbook* by Stewart Henderson, copyright © 1989, and used by permission of Hodder & Stoughton Ltd., PO Box 700, Dunton Green, Sevenoaks, Kent, TN13 27A.

'The last enemy' was taken from *Assembled in Britain* by Stewart Henderson, copyright © 1986, published by Marshall Pickering, and used by permission of Harper Collins Publishers Ltd., 8 Grafton Street, London, W1X 3LA.

'Speak' by Evangeline Paterson was taken from *The Least Thing*, ed. Angela Topping, copyright © 1989, published by Stride/ Greenbelt Files and used by permission of Stride, 37 Portland Street, Exeter, Devon, EX1 2EG.

'Mr Adam' and 'Somewhere in suburbia' are taken from *Frogs and Princes* by Mike Starkey, copyright © 1987 and used by permission of Monarch Publications Ltd., 1 St Anne's Road, Eastbourne, East Sussex, BN21 3UN.

'Five hundred million pounds', 'The news and weather' and 'Whose grave is the ocean' are taken from *Up To Date* by Steve Turner, copyright © 1983, and used by permission of Hodder & Stoughton Ltd.

'Join what?' by Steven Waling is taken from *The Least Thing*, ed. Angela Topping, copyright © 1989, and used by permission of Stride.

Biographies

Fraser Grace lives in Birmingham, where he works as a writer and dramatist. He has performed his poetry at many national events including Greenbelt, Spring Harvest and the Edinburgh Festival Fringe, and published his first collection, *Poems For The Hard Of Hearing* in 1985. He is also the author of a book on drama, and two books of fiction, while more recent verse has fuelled his one-man show, 'Angels, Ghosts and Mortal Men'.

Stewart Henderson was born in Liverpool in 1952 and began performing his poetry while in his teens. Since then he has toured all over the UK, the USA and Holland, and has appeared at Greenbelt Festival (of which he is a director), Spring Harvest and the Edinburgh Festival Fringe. His poetry has been broadcast on both TV and Radio, and published in two major collections, *Assembled In Britain* (1986), and *A Giant's Scrapbook* (1989), as well as in numerous booklets, magazines and anthologies.

Gerald Kells, free-lance writer and committed Green has published prose and poetry in various magazines including *Strait*, *Cross Rhythms*, and *Christian Magazine*, and is featured in *Contemporary Christian Verse*. He has also written sketches for BBC Radio 4's 'Arnold Brown and Company', and is Artistic Director of the Half-Baked Drama Company.

Gerard Kelly is a full-time Schools Worker, currently based in Exeter. He has performed at Greenbelt and Spring Harvest and at National Youth For Christ events, as well as using poetry extensively in school assemblies, church services and youth events. His first solo collection, *Rebel Without Applause*, was published in 1990.

Rupert Loydell's poetry has appeared in many magazines, anthologies and books, both in Britain and abroad. Recently his work has been featured in *Acumen*, *The Green Book*, *Ostinato*, and *Outposts* magazines. His books include *Fill these days* (selected poems), *The Fantasy Kid* (illustrated stories and poems for children), and *Pitched At Silence* (a book of improvised jazz poems). Rupert is editor of Stride Publications, is married and lives in Exeter.

Millie Murray was born in London of Jamaican parents and is a qualified general and psychiatric nurse.

To date, Millie has published three novels: *Kiesha* (1988), *Lady A – A teenage D.J.* (1989), and *All About Jas* (1990). A number of her short stories have also been published and broadcast, including 'A Blessing in Disguise', which has been reprinted by Longman's for use in GCSE classes.

Evangeline Paterson was born in Limavady, Northern Ireland, grew up in Dublin, and now lives in Newcastle with her husband, John, who is a Geography Professor.

Evangeline has published several collections of her poetry, including *Bringing The Water Hyacinth To Africa*, a 'selected poems' published in 1983 by Taxus. She has also been widely anthologized, and is featured in Paladin's *New British Poetry*.

Born and brought up on a farm in East Kent, **Peggy Poole** has spent most of her life beside the Dee estuary on Merseyside. Widely published in poetry magazines, she has had several collections published, is the author of a number of children's books and an adult novel, and is also a freelance broadcaster/journalist. Her work is included in *New Christian Poetry*, published by Collins in 1990, while her fifth solo collection was also published in 1990.

Mark Reaney was born in Liverpool where he works as a writer. He has published three volumes of poems, including *A World*

Apart, in aid of Tear Fund, and *Taken As Read.* Mark has read his work at the Greenbelt and Crossfire Festivals, in many pubs and clubs in the Merseyside area, and on local radio. He is married to Gill.

Mike Starkey works as a newsreader and reporter in commercial radio. Based in Cambridge, he is the author of *Born To Shop,* a witty analysis of modern consumerism from a Christian perspective. As a poet he has performed his verse at Greenbelt and on TV, and published his first collection, *Frogs & Princes* in 1987. Mike is married to author Naomi Starkey, and they have one son, Joel.

Michele Taylor trained as a teacher and is now Artistic Director for Footprints Theatre Company in Nottingham. Her work involves performing and leading workshops as well as writing and devising theatre projects for the Company. Other writing credits include poetry, articles, short stories and a Ph.D. in medical ethics.

Steve Turner began writing poetry in 1965 and gave his first public reading in 1968. He has published three books of poetry – *Tonight We Will Fake Love* (1974), *Nice And Nasty* (1980) and *Up To Date* (1983). Reviewing *Up To Date, New Musical Express* commented; 'When you've read this book you feel as if he's given you something positive to hang on to in a world so certain of its uncertainties.'

A new collection of poetry is due in 1991.

Steven Waling was born in Accrington, Lancashire in 1958 and has been published in a number of magazines and anthologies, including *The Least Thing* (Stride/Greenbelt Files) and *Christian Magazine.*

Steven's booklet, entitled *Riding Shotgun* won the Smith/Doorstop pamphlet competition in 1988. He is currently editing a magazine called *Brando's Hat,* and attending his local Quaker meeting.

Alex Warner works as a gardener in Stalybridge, Cheshire, where he lives with his wife Beverly and their three children. Alex was a member of the *Stand & Deliver* performance poetry team based in Tameside, and is a founder member of the Stalybridge Writer's Group. He has produced two collections of poetry, *Not Quite Human* and *Pennine Peaks*, has been published in a variety of magazines, and is featured in *New Christian Poetry* published in 1990 by Collins.

Author Index